D1598337

It's Not Putting Me Down
It's Lifting Me Up

A Guilt-Free Guide
to
End-of-Life Decisions for Pets

Excerpts from the book
"Only Gone from Your Sight"
For veterinary and aftercare professionals,
counselors, and anyone who loves someone who is
preparing for or suffers from the loss of a pet.

KATE McGAHAN, LMSW

This book belongs to

_____

In Memory of

_____

*A prayer was sent into the world
to comfort someone who
was needing love. It landed here
and now this book loves you.*

_____

"Let there be no sorrow
for one day we will meet
in a place where there are
no more goodbyes."
–Jack McAfghan

TABLE OF CONTENTS

INTRODUCTION

Dear One,

I see how you grieve. You think your heart is broken and that you will never be happy again. You are facing the loss of someone near and dear to you, and it happens to be your pet. Those who never loved a pet the way you have loved yours cannot fathom the magnitude of it. This is a unique once-in-a-lifetime love affair. A love without limits. All the time. Forever and ever.

You think no one understands, but I do. My name is Jack. I was born in a puppy mill and I never dreamed I would have a beautiful life, but I sure did! I was so lucky the day she came through the gate and chose me. I was only 10 weeks old and the day I met her my life changed forever. Those of us who have had a loving home with a best friend who loves us as much as we love them, we are blessed! I know that you are one of those loving people because that is why you are reading this book. I know you that you came here to find peace and understanding in your loss. You are reading this book because you have loved and been loved so much and you wonder how you'll make it through the grief.

There is someone else who loves you: the one who gave you this book because they knew you needed to feel better. It is one of the most difficult things in a human lifetime to say goodbye to a loyal best friend. Stay with me here and I will prove to you that it's not goodbye at all. It's not the end.

Join me on a guided tour through the world of grief. In the pages that follow I will help you to prepare for inevitable loss and difficult end of life decisions. We will discuss memorial ideas and ultimately how to move forward into living life fully, perhaps even opening your heart to love again. Our primary book "Only Gone from Your Sight" expands on this book by walking you through the five stages of grief, teaching the power of signs and dreams, how to talk with your children and other pets about the loss ...and more. The small book that you are holding is specifically written for those who do not read or don't want to read but who need to prepare for and cope with the end of life.

I will be referring to the words "Dead" "Death" "Die" and "Dying." I do it for the sake of simplicity but the fact is if you have read my other books you know there is no such thing as death. My definition of death is not the death of the spirit but the freeing of the spirit of the soul. The soul is what lives on long beyond this earthly life. It is the part of each one of us that lives forever. It is connected to everyone we love no matter what, no matter where we are.

As your Rainbow Bridge representative, please join me on this special journey. Don't be surprised if you feel the presence of your best friend here with us, for we are all here beside you, only gone from your view as you read these words, as you cry your tears and one day as you smile your gentle smile for the memory of us. We bring you the comfort of a friend who loves and supports you no matter what. There is no judgment here. There is no criticism. There is only love and understanding. We are devoted to you forever. We are never far away. It's our turn to take you for a little walk...along the edge of the Rainbow. Come. Everything is going to be okay. You'll see.

Love, Jack

RAINBOW BRIDGE

Just this side of heaven is a place called
Rainbow Bridge.
When an animal dies that has been especially
close to someone here,
that pet goes to Rainbow Bridge.
There are meadows and hills
for all of our special friends
so they can run and play together.
There is plenty of food, water and sunshine,
and our friends are warm and comfortable.
All the animals who had been ill and old are
restored to health and vigor. Those who were
hurt or maimed are made whole and strong
again, just as we remember them in
our dreams of days and times gone by.
The animals are happy and content,
except for one small thing;
they each miss someone very special to them,

who had to be left behind.
They all run and play together, but the day
comes when one suddenly stops and looks into
the distance. His bright eyes are intent.
His eager body quivers.
Suddenly
he begins to run from the group,
flying over the green grass,
his legs carrying him faster and faster.
You have been spotted, and when you and
your special friend finally meet,
you cling together in joyous reunion,
never to be parted again.
The happy kisses rain upon your face;
your hands again caress the beloved head,
and you look once more into the trusting eyes
of your pet, so long gone from your life
but never absent from your heart.

Then you cross Rainbow Bridge together.

Author Unknown

NOT 'JUST' A PET

*It was hard for friends to know how to comfort
her. After all, I had been like her child, her
boyfriend, her husband and her best friend all
wrapped up in one furry package. Pets can
become like family members especially for those
who do not have a family of their own.*
<u>*Jack McAfghan: Reflections, Chapter 73*</u>

You might find it difficult to open up your
heart and talk with most people because you
fear they might think you crazy for loving me
more than you've loved any human. All too
many who deeply grieve the loss of a pet have
been 'reassured' by a statement from a well-
meaning friend, "It's just a dog/ cat/ horse/
hamster/ rabbit/ parakeet... You can get
another one." Forgive them for they know not
what they do or what they say.

Even other animal owners might not
understand. Some people who own pets are
only master, not friend, and they miss out on
the best parts of the human-animal bond. If
only they could see that we are there to teach
them and to give them the love that has
otherwise been missing in their lives. The love
most humans do not know how to give...or
receive. These are the people who might laugh
or sneer at you now when you call me your
soulmate because they never have heard of

such a thing. They think that all soulmates are romantic relationships between two people, not loving relationships between two beings, two friends, two soul travelers such as us. Pity them for what they do not know. Pity them that they cannot treat anyone else better than they treat themselves. Pity them for the love they've never had or recognized.

Love is chemistry beyond our control. When true love comes into your life it can transform you in the most extraordinary ways and change everything you ever believed in. You are never sure where true love is going to come from and it can be quite a surprise when it comes from your pet.

While it may sound strange that someone can grieve more deeply for a pet than for a human, there is a certain undeniable depth that comes from sharing a life of unconditional love. It doesn't matter how many legs I have or how many you have, it's a soul connection. No matter how we found each other, no matter how long we have been together, it is a relationship like no other. I have given you the kind of love that takes humans a lifetime to learn, if they ever learn. I know the power of love and I want to give it to you. It is the most powerful force in the universe. I came into this world to give true love to you and to draw true love out of you. How many people in your life do that?

Of course people do the best they can, giving and receiving their imperfect human love. There are a few special people on earth who are very old souls and they are capable of loving at a very deep level. They give the highest form of love; love that is divinely pure, honest and unconditional. It holds the loved one more precious than oneself. It sacrifices without complaint, without resentment, without keeping score. It gives and gives and expects nothing in return. It's the same kind of love that I have given to you. I came into the world to love and be loved and I chose you. Love is why I came here. You are the reason I came. My love has become a part of you but you don't seem to understand that yet. When I am gone you don't seem to know who you are without me. You don't know your identity without me. I will teach you. I will teach you through life and I will teach you through death. I will teach you that love never dies.

When you love from the depths of the soul in your heart, you are never apart from the one you love no matter how far away you seem to be. Even when I am gone from your sight, I am never gone from your heart. We live in the heart of one another for eternity, beyond the reaches of this world. The love runs deep. That's why it hurts so much for so long when we have to say "goodbye". That's also why you will get through this. Our love runs so deep that nothing can touch it, no, not even death. Our love will win. It always does when it is true.

I tried to comfort her. I spoke in a voice she could not hear. Her grief and sadness drowned me out. I wanted to tell her what I have always known. That life is but a dream leading to love. Love, more powerful than her fear could ever be. Love cannot be destroyed. It grows and grows until it is stronger than death.
<u>*Jack McAfghan: Reflections, Chapter 72*</u>

Soulmates change all the rules in the game of life. We have been brought together, you and me, by a common destiny. We have known each other before and we will know each other again. I will continue to transform you from beyond the grave and help you to see that love is more valuable and powerful than anything else.

There will be others who will not understand this kind of love. They will raise their eyebrows as they stand in judgment of you and comment how silly it is that you loved me this much. Don't worry about them. I feel sorry for them. They obviously have never encountered a soulmate of their own or they would know better. They would know that traditional rules do not apply when a match is made in Heaven. Once you know this kind of love you will never question love again. You'll know it when you see it. You'll know it when you feel it. You will never be confused by something that is something else.

ANTICIPATORY GRIEF

Death. I wish the word could be removed from the vocabulary and from the dictionary. It simply does not exist, except in the human mind that was taught that it does exist. People think they are a body and they come to believe that when the body dies, everything they are will die too. It's not true. The soul lives on. The soul of consciousness exists not only in the body but outside of the body too. We are all souls that cannot be contained or limited by time or space or the physical body. For souls there is no death.
Return from Rainbow Bridge, Chapter 13

When you brought me into your life it changed everything for both of us. It was not so long ago we were still traveling the world together thinking we'd live forever.

All the adventures come to pass and then seemingly out of the blue one day something happens that, once again, changes everything. Life will never be the same. The fear sets in. The threat of loss permeates your being and taints the world around you, disrupting everything. It's all you can think about, the impending loss of me. It's another kind of adventure that we will come to share. When something big changes your life, it's because you have something big to learn. You learned

9

from my coming and you'll learn from my going.

Living with fear and the ache in your heart as you watch me decline, you wonder how you'll ever live without me. Perhaps you have already made some difficult choices on my behalf. Costly medications. Challenging treatments. Surgeries. Countless fears and days and nights on end filled with worry for me.

You look back on the investment of life you have made with me. From the early training to the bond of love we've created through life's ups and downs, you've became a part of me and I've become a part of you. That bond of love we've created together will never be broken even though I will soon be gone. Oh but not gone at all, Only Gone from Your Sight.

Anticipatory grief begins the moment you realize that my death is inevitable, that there's no going back to the way things used to be. We will not be discussing the five stages of grief as we do in our fourth book but you will probably go through a mini-version of all five during this pre-grief process, during your anticipation of what is ahead. Your life shifts dramatically because you now anticipate my death and must prepare for it. But how on earth do you prepare for something such as this?

"Oh no, no, no," you Deny. "It cannot be true!" You are Angry. "It's just not fair!" You Bargain. "Certainly there must be more tests that can be done!" You become Depressed when you learn that there are no more tests; there is nothing that can be done. There is little time left.

You learn that you have no control over the situation and you are ultimately forced to accept the circumstances. You imagine your world without me in it. Hesitantly you begin to picture what your life will be like and, while unpleasant, the visualization of it is like a little rehearsal. It's like a preview that prepares you just a little bit for when the time comes. It's all predesigned so that you can begin to accept the fact that I am dying.

Some of you begin this process of grief long before there is need for concern. This usually stems from your fear of the future, your attachment to me, and an ultimate Not Wanting and Not Knowing What to Do when the time comes. It stems from the fear that you can't make it on your own without me. It's the resistance of having to face the living of life without me in it. Death forces change. It's the final stage of growth for the one who is dying and it is a teacher that forces the growth of the one who remains. Most people are averse to change and they tend to cling to old ways of being in an effort to try to keep things the same. But they can't keep things the same. So they grieve just thinking about it.

It isn't necessarily healthy, the clinging and this feeling of need that you have, but it's understandable. This early phase is by design. It gives you time. It makes you extra appreciative of what you have now. I am so grateful because I know you always appreciated me, but when you know the end of something is coming, you don't take anything for granted. When you know your time is short, each moment is precious and with each moment comes the opportunity to say what needs to be said and to express your deepest love and appreciation to the one who will be leaving soon. Or to the one who loves the one who is leaving soon, if you happen to be the one who is dying.

Believe it or not, this anticipatory time is a gift in disguise. Not everyone is given time to prepare for loss. Some experience loss through trauma, accident, or sudden death. It happens so fast that you don't know what hit you. You never had a chance to say goodbye. You could not have anticipated it. There was no way to prepare for it. You did not have the "luxury" of this phase of experience called Anticipatory Grief.

If you have not learned this, we now have this opportunity for me to teach you to look at your life and mine In the Moment. To help you to see what you have now and what you will not have later and to make the most of each and every moment we have together in the meantime.

I've been waiting for you. Come with me. Let's live In the Moment together...

FACING THE INEVITABLE

We've received the diagnosis and it's not good news. There's no hope for survival. It's overwhelming and it takes only a moment to overload your mind. You can feel so blindsided at the time that you stop functioning. You just do whatever you are told to do. This phenomenon often takes place at the veterinarian's office when the diagnosis, with poor prognosis, is first presented. Being overwhelmed by it is not your fault; it's the shock of the situation. You nod your head and passively say, "Okay" to everything. Even the things you don't quite understand. You don't make the most of communicating your feelings, stating your needs or asking your questions. There's nothing more that can be done. You see no way out; you're between a rock and a hard place. You don't ask how much it will cost. You are thrown into a state of shock and denial, blinded like a deer in headlights.

Fear takes over. You come to look at everything through the filter of your fear and you feel disempowered. You find you can't make clear decisions and you default to someone, anyone, who will make those decisions for you. You feel that you have lost control and you give it over to the only one who seems willing to take it. You give it to the one with the clearest mind. The expert. The one we have come to trust over our years together. Our veterinarian.

Pre-grief is already kicking in, the shock, the numbness. You're not yourself. You don't think and act the way you normally would. The problem is that later on, you will feel guilty because you won't understand why you didn't have the strength or the know-how to fight the decision or to express your preferences. The shock has disempowered you and you may even feel anger towards the one who encouraged you to make the particular decision, all because you couldn't...even though you agreed to it.

You go into a state of pre-grief shock because you realize that everything is different now. Most things are out of your hands. You have already Shut Down. You aren't up for a fight. You are too overwhelmed trying to figure out how to surrender to things that are beyond your control. For some of you, all that's left is the power of prayer and the hope for a miracle.

You've always been so busy but our days together here are winding down now. The wonderful thing for me is that once you slow down and really focus on what is going on between you and me, you are finally Living In The Moment. I've been trying to teach you this all of my life while your busy world kept you spinning.

The most important thing you can do for me in these final days is to sit quietly with me.

BE with me. If we have not already learned how to speak Heart to Heart, we can learn now. Because I do not have a voice to tell you, my heart will help your heart to know what I want and what I need in the days ahead. This is the "language" we can practice now. This is the language that will ultimately help us to transcend the space between us when I am gone from your sight. It's how I will speak to you. It's how I always spoke to you but you never really heard me because you didn't know how. You weren't tuned in. Let's learn now. We will get through this together with the power of the love in our hearts. We have time.

Let's practice. Put one hand on my heart and the other on yours. Sit quietly with me, breathe with me, feel our hearts beating together. Look into my eyes. We are building a foundation of understanding, heart to heart. It will be good for both of us. The heart is the bridge that connects us now and it is the bridge that will connect us when I am gone. The bridge that joins your heart to mine IS the Rainbow Bridge! If I have already made my transition, call me to come to you anyway and I will come to you. Sit with me even though I am gone from your sight. Have faith. I am still with you; sit with me now.

Someday whenever the world gets to be too much, even when I'm gone, put your hands on your heart because that is where I will be. I will remind you that your power is in your heart, not in your head.

END OF LIFE DECISIONS
WHAT IS NOT GROWING IS DYING

I learned that Blanca felt totally helpless. She was tired of living. She wanted to be free of her cumbersome body. She felt trapped. She loved her family but she suffered from a deep and painful longing to return Home. Her heavenly Master was calling for her but her earthly master was clinging to her. It was painful for her to be pulled in two different directions.
<u>*Jack McAfghan: Reflections, Chapter 52*</u>

It can be challenging and surreal, that time before death when you know for certain that our time together is brief. The anticipation of the inevitable change is typically harder than the change itself because the anticipation of something keeps you out of the power of the moment while you live in fear of the future.

The clock of earthly life ticks off our remaining moments together. We have reached the point where you must make some big decisions on my behalf. It is a precious time for you and me: the final days, hours, minutes, moments...It is a time of shared learning through new feelings and experience. It is my final opportunity to teach you the importance of living with me in the moment. There are so few moments left. I will help you to make the most of every bit of time we have together. It is a time to share our love and affection and it is a time to communicate, your heart to mine, my heart to yours. Like I taught you.

Ask me what I want. I will tell you. You can see the way I carry myself. You can see it in my eyes. It's the light that shines out at you from them that will tell you everything you need to know. My love for you has kept my eyes clear and bright for a very long time. If you see that my eyes have dimmed, it's because some of my light is already shining on the other side of the rainbow. It is because I am preparing for my departure to a forever land where love never dies. Where you and I will ultimately come together to live for eternity.

As I decline, death does not take me all at once. You may find that I leave a little bit at a time. Maybe I won't be as steady on my feet or I get so tired that I just can't stay awake without falling fast asleep again. It is a message to you that I am increasingly "tired" of living this way. I might start having accidents in the house because my systems are shutting down. When I stop eating towards the end of life, it is often my way of telling you to "stop" too. It is the one thing I still have control over, whether I eat or not. It's the one clear way I can communicate with you that I do not want to keep nourishing a life that no longer works for me. There is a different kind of nourishment I need now. As much as I love you, the time comes when we have to give up the fight and surrender to the next journey.

17

Just like the light in my eyes will tell you if I am leaving, my mind might stray to the other side too. I will be less focused on what is going on around me, more focused on where it is that I am going. You'll look at me and it may seem as if I am not there, but I am. I am just learning some important things from those on the other side who need to speak, their heart to mine, to help me to know what I can expect as I make my transition. Even if my eyes are not focused upon you, I am still here. I am still very aware of your presence and your state of mind. I can still hear you. I can hear you and feel you through all the final moments and beyond...even if I seem to be unconscious.

......Another shift has taken place. Your heart is in your throat because you see my eyes have lost their shine. My light has dimmed. You are now observing each and every detail. Your all-knowing heart sags within your chest. You're bracing yourself because now you know that it's true. Now you know that I will be leaving you soon. I am already separating from the pain and oh it feels so much better.

You are suddenly intensely aware of how little control you have. You fast-forward your mind wondering how you will get through this. The fears come. Fears for you. Fears for me. Once again you move out of the love and into the fear. You forget about living in the moment and instead you worry about the future; you fear what is coming. You don't know what to

18

do or how you'll handle it. You think you are not qualified to make end of life decisions for me. They are tough decisions that weigh heavy. You feel that my life is in your hands. You don't want to make these choices all by yourself. You don't need to.

Consult with our veterinarian who will present all the possibilities for my treatment and care. Make sure it can't be fixed. Explore natural remedies. Be open to traditional care. If you are more comfortable getting a second opinion, get a second opinion. Do whatever you can to preserve my comfort and my quality of life. Don't go into a lot of debt to try to save me through expensive procedures, especially if I am older and have been slowing down anyway. I will be saved soon enough when I make my journey into Heaven.

If our vet has done everything possible and my quality of life is still compromised, I must depend on you to decide what's best for me. Put yourself in my place. How does it feel to live like this? In the garden of life what is not growing is dying. So if I am declining, a decision to prolong my life is really only prolonging my dying. If I am running low and my quality of life is compromised, please be willing to let me go. You will understand this more if you have experienced the pain and discomfort that can come with age or if you have ever sought relief from your own pain because of disease or injury. There are worse things than to cross the bridge into the peace that is Heaven. In fact, there is really nothing better. I know it's hard for you to face my death. It's harder for you than it is for me. I am not grieving. You are. You do not grieve for me; you grieve for you for the loss of me. There is no loss in this scenario for me. I will have the peace that is Heaven and I will still have you. I will have everything.

It takes love to hold on when you want to let go. It takes love to let go when you want to hold on. As we move forward together, tell me you love me. Tell me you'll miss me. Tell me you'll grieve and that you will also heal. Reassure me that you'll try to love again. Leave nothing unsaid. Stay by my side whenever possible. Most of all be willing to let me go when it's time to let me go. Give me permission to go so that it is easier for me.

Explore the possibility of care through a pet hospice if there is one in your area. They are invaluable and they will do everything possible to keep me comfortable through my final days. They will also help you to oversee the aftercare arrangements and support you through the process. The thought of having someone there for you even now comforts me. I don't ever want you to feel alone.

If I cannot go on my own terms, I trust you to help me. I know you'll do the right thing when you listen to your heart. The ideal time to let me go is before chronic pain further compromises my quality of life. Let me go on my passage before I have too much pain, before I lose my dignity, before I suffer and create memories of suffering. Those are the memories your mind will tend to go to first and those are the memories I do not want you to focus on. I want you to remember the good times, the healthy happy times when we were in our prime. Oh there were so many of them!

Because it's not your area of expertise, death and letting go, you might think that you need a mediator to help you to make the final decision. But the truth is, I am your point of expertise. Nobody knows me like you do. You can hire a good communicator, pet whisperer or counselor...or you can do it yourself. Have you forgotten? You and me, heart to heart? You forgot because you moved out of the moment with me and back into the fear.

Shhhh. Be with me now. Quietly look into my eyes for they will speak to you. The eyes are the windows to the soul; your soul is directly connected to mine. That fact will never change. Tune into my soul and you will know how I feel. The soul understands everything, one for the other. I will show you that I want to stay or let you know if it's time for me to go. Keep the focus on the love in your heart not the fear in your head. Put yourself in my place. I know you love me. Every situation is different and you must do what you must do for you and for me. I have always trusted you to do what is best for me within the choices that we have.

I may have four legs or wings or scales or fins but I understand everything, my heart to yours. Make the most of this time for when all is said and done these are the moments life is made of and you will need to reflect back on this time and know you did your very best, that you made a difference to me in my final days. You did. You made all the difference in everything for me.

PREPARING FOR THE PASSAGE

I didn't want to leave her
but I was obedient first and foremost.
I knew I had to go Home.
She was sending me…and I was being called.
<u>*Jack McAfghan: Reflections, Chapter 65*</u>

You've taken the first step. You've made THE DECISION. You've scheduled THE APPOINTMENT with the vet. It's on the calendar in black and white. It's real. No matter how much time we have, you are now well aware that our time together is fleeting at best. You want to spend as much time with me as possible.

When humans get very old and frail, they are lucky if they have a doctor who, as he orders up hospice comfort care for them, takes away all restrictions. Do the same for me because you will be glad later that you did. Looking back, you've given me everything! You gave me so much that I never wanted for anything I didn't have. Now it's time to really spoil me rotten!

Let me sleep on the bed with you. Give me all the ice cream and cookies that I want. Diabetes is no longer a fear for me. Nothing is really. There isn't any time left for that. Some hamburger from the dinner table would be lovely, the table you never fed me from because you are such a good master. Let me rest or let me play. Let me dig holes in the dirt or stay outside later than I normally would. A special trip to say goodbye to our friends at the park, a final farewell to our favorite beach, one last lounge on the front lawn. I'm probably not up for too many trips, but you know best. You can ask me and you will know by the wag in my tail or the absence of it – or the look in my eye or the tweak in my ear if that's one of the things I want to do. Mostly I just want to be with you. If you can take a day or two off from work that would be so wonderful for me and for you too. Whatever I want, please do it for me because it will all mean more than you realize when I am gone from your sight.

This is my time. I am well aware of what is happening because you told me, your heart to mine. It makes me happy that I am finally going Home and that I have your blessings in doing so. It's hard to leave you but I knew all along this would happen. I knew from the day we met. I also know that I will be seeing you again in time that will pass in the blink of an eye. Please promise me that you'll try to stay focused on the times we shared when life was good; when you never paid a second thought that it would come to this.

Some people delay and cling because they can't let go. Don't make me wait too long. I'm ready anytime. When all is said and done, more people feel they waited too long than those who felt they let go too soon. Our vet will help you to determine the best time and the best way. Don't forget to talk with me along the way and let me know what is happening so I can be better prepared too.

If you beg me not to leave, it will be painful for me because there is a complex mix of energies taking place. The physical body itself continues in its determination to live. It has never done anything else. It wants to keep living so it works against death. There is also an unseen and commanding but loving force that pulls me to the other side. All of a sudden I feel the force of you asking me not to go. Not to leave you. You don't need to say anything for me to feel this for I can read your thoughts. While I know I must go, I will still choose to suffer any amount of pain in order to be obedient to you. I am caught betwixt and between and yet my passing is inevitable. This is why it is important for you to give me permission to go for if you do not, you will look back and feel guilty for causing me the pain of your resistance. I don't want you to feel guilty because you aren't. Yet your potential anguish is so much worse and more painful than my temporary pain could ever be.

Kate would often look tentatively at my older sheltie sister Grady when she was sleeping to see if she was still breathing. Every night. Every morning. Naptimes. She would brace herself, hoping...fearing... Perhaps like you, Kate didn't want to have to make any decisions. She just wanted Grady to go to sleep on her own and not wake up. She waited while Grady declined more and more. It was a very passive technique because Kate didn't want to make the wrong decision so she made no decision at all.

That which you avoid will keep coming back to you in order to heal whatever is getting in the way of your growth. Sometimes decision-making is a part of a person's growth. Kate always avoided making decisions that impacted others in her life. So here was Grady, her teacher, giving her the opportunity to step up to the plate. It's another gift, the gift of growth. The way I see it, you really can't make a wrong decision if you take the judgment out of it.

Kate had been waiting for God to call for Grady who suffered year after year, but God just didn't call for Grady. After awhile she got to thinking that maybe this was just a test of her love. Maybe it was a test to see if she loved Grady enough to let her go.
Jack McAfghan: Reflections, Chapter 19

You've scheduled THE APPOINTMENT, but wait! I'm having a really good day! I am so active that it makes you question whether you are doing the right thing. It can be very confusing and may put you into a sort of agony as you proceed to second-guess your decision. Please don't cancel the appointment. It is just that I know. I know it is the Last Hurrah in this life of mine and I want to make the most of it. It is easy for me to have more energy because I am so happy about all of this. I'm so relieved. I know I am going Home soon where I will be free of pain and limitation. In the meantime I will purr and wag my tail and run around as best I can to show you how happy I am that I have shared this life with you and how blessed I am that you are the one I love! It's my final Swan Song. This is how I want you to remember me. I do not want you to remember me as anything but happy.

You cannot turn back the clock. You cannot change the circumstances. You never could change them. They were set in Destiny, in the fate of the Rainbow Timetable. You need to love yourself as much as I love you and forgive yourself everything. You are not guilty of anything. You loved me and love is always enough.
<u>Return from Rainbow Bridge</u>

"THE APPOINTMENT"
EUTHANASIA

There are not enough words in the English language to describe the experience of this. Death is more than life. Humans put their animals "to sleep" when it's really waking them up. Everybody has it backwards.
<u>*Jack McAfghan: Reflections, Chapter 68*</u>

It is the most unselfish act in all of life to let one go that we have found beloved.

You don't want to think about it but it's the first thing on your mind. You say, "We made THE APPOINTMENT." You avoid the word "euthanasia" because it makes everything too real. It is a beautiful word, really. It is Greek for "easy death" and it is true, there is no easier death than this. It is unfortunate that, once again, people are so afraid of death in all its forms that they find it so difficult even when the time of death is peaceful.

So many say they put their pets 'down' when they are really lifting them up. It's true. Nobody likes to be put down. 'Putting To Sleep' is a much better term even though it's still kind of inaccurate. Nonetheless, whatever words you use to describe it, you are helping me. Don't question your decision again. It's the most loving thing you can do, to help me on my way Home.

To best be prepared, be sure to ask our vet to describe to you what you can expect. Find out what our options are – if it can take place at home or at the clinic. The right vet will calmly reassure us and accommodate our preferences and comfort levels. Kate had Grady put to sleep in our car under a shady tree outside the vet clinic. Grady always got very anxious about going to the clinic but she loved being in the car; she had spent so much time there making miles of memories. Our vet didn't make house calls at the time but more and more vets do now so that we don't have to be overly anxious or afraid. They make it possible to have an easy transition from the comfort of our very own bed. We can just close our eyes at home and open them in our heavenly Home. It's so perfect.

It is very important for me for everything to go as smoothly as possible during the appointment. Be sure that you are comfortable with the procedure and the cost that you and our vet have agreed upon. Hopefully our regular vet will be available because s/he is a familiar friend to me and it helps to know that s/he loves me too. I hope that the trusted staff will support you in your grief when I am gone.

If you can, plan on being there at the appointment with me and staying with me until it's done. It will not take long. If you need to bring someone with you for emotional support, don't hesitate to ask someone you love and trust to be there with you. Maybe it's even someone who loves me too, someone I would love to have beside us in my final moments. I was always the one who was there, so knowing that someone is there for you will reassure me too. You may also need someone to drive you home because you don't know what your state of mind will be later. How you handle this last visit is very personal and you must do what is best for you and for me.

The most important thing to remember is to help to create an environment for me as calm as can be under the circumstances. Being surrounded by love always alleviates pain and suffering. When we love and feel loved we are more immune to feeling the effects of physical or emotional discomfort. Love is a powerful force. My love for you and yours for me will get us through this appointment.

On the other hand, if you are crying and carrying on, it will make things more difficult for me and it might be best for you not to be present. You know how it always upset me when you were upset. Our final moments on earth impact the entry into our next life and it is always best if these moments can be as comforting as possible. If you are as calm as you can be and can just stay in your feeling of love for me, I can handle any tears that might come. It's your love I need to feel. Try to stay in the love and not in the fear. Really BE with me in the final moments. Like I taught you.

If you ultimately choose not to be present, I understand. Give me your love before they close the door and if you can it would be nice if you could spend some time afterwards with me, for closure for yourself and for me. If you cannot bear that, I understand. I am not in the body on the blanket on the table anyway. I am already on my way across the bridge to Heaven.

Do not stand at my grave and weep,
I am not there; I do not sleep.
I am a thousand winds that blow,
I am the diamond glints on snow,
I am the sun on ripened grain,
I am the gentle autumn rain.
When you awaken in the morning's hush
I am the swift uplifting rush
Of quiet birds in circling flight.
I am the soft star-shine at night.
Do not stand at my grave and cry,
I am not there; I did not die.

~Mary Elizabeth Frye

The surgery I required put Kate between a rock and a hard place.

"If he dies on the table it could be a blessing," she said, "He could comfortably just fade away."

I would like to clarify that whether one is "put under" for surgery or "put under" for euthanasia, there is no pain. It is a most gentle transition. The difference is that after surgery we are brought back and in euthanasia we are allowed to go.

I didn't die on the table. It wasn't supposed to be that easy for her. We still had more to do together. The most important part of our life together would come during the week that followed. I was blessed that I could die at home with her by my side. Death is the final stage of growth and she learned more in those last five days than she had learned in all our years together. Her love for me reached to the sky and would change the way she would come to look at everything. Had it happened any other way, any other time, you would not be reading this book or any of the others.

I had to suffer for had I not she'd be clinging to me even now, wanting me to stay with her. It hurts when someone won't let go. Not only do we have to leave, we must tear ourselves from one who clings. My suffering has served a purpose. She desperately wanted me to stay but because her love for me was greater than her need for me, she wanted me to be free of pain and this made it easier for her to let me go.

Some of us need to suffer so that we seek relief, to be free from our own suffering. Otherwise we would never ever leave your side! In death there is much more going on than meets the eye. It's a fine balance of many things. Each piece of the puzzle needs to fit so all the other kazillions of pieces in the universe will fit too. All of us are connected all the time.

Even in death we are living out our destinies together. All of our lives fit together like giant puzzle pieces. It's all about being in the right place at the right time. We are all continually connected to countless other souls who need us to fulfill our destiny...and we must stay on schedule.

Suddenly time stands still.

You. Me. The vet. The room.

...An IV infusion and in just a few moments a drop of my heavy head...and in that moment peace comes at last. That long, well-deserved sleep after a hard day's work. When it is over and all is stillness, all pain and suffering are gone. It is done. I am already at peace and my new journey has begun. A journey that still includes you.

Remember when you would come home from work after a long and difficult day? You were tired already when the day began and you thought that it would never end. But it did. You cross the threshold and drop into bed and fall into a deep refreshing sleep. Later upon waking you feel so rested and relaxed that you don't want to move. You don't want to spoil the moment. You don't want to wake up just yet. That's what it's like for me. It's been a long road and even though I love you very much, I am tired. I am asking you to let me sleep now.

You have done the most thoughtful and humane thing for me possible. You gave me the final act of love. You set your own desires aside to honor what was best for me. You allowed me to run free over the Rainbow Bridge into a wonderful world where there is no pain or discomfort of any kind. It is a world that we will share together in a day that will pass when the time is right.

Please realize that my suffering was short-lived compared to the life I lived and loved with you. All of that life is but a blink of an eye when compared to the eternal life I am living now. It was just a tiny moment in time. You'll see when we are back together again. You'll see how it all works and you will look back and say how foolish you were to worry so. But worry, it's the human condition. It cannot be helped.

"Why?" You demand, "Why did he have to suffer?" "He never did anything to hurt anyone!" "He didn't deserve this!"

The fact is...it is not for you to judge or decide. Keep in mind that death itself is not painful - on the contrary - although the illness or injury preceding it might be. Death is just death. Death is a letting go and there is no better feeling once you are ready.

If I had pain or suffering, there must have been a good reason. Pain is a messenger; it tells you that it's time for change. It pushes you until you have no choice but to address it. You forget that there is a power over all things with the final say in everything. The fact is:

there IS a reason for everything. Even for the suffering of an innocent being. Sometimes the only positive thing you have to hold onto is the fact that I suffer no more.

It's true. I suffer no more yet you continue to suffer the memory of my suffering. I am waiting for you to heal. Can you remember how heartsick you felt when you witnessed my suffering? It's the same for me. I don't want to see you suffer either! I am waiting for you to let go of the suffering...the suffering that no longer exists except in your own mind.

I really wanted to stay with her but my heavenly Master's voice is strong. I knew then why I had to suffer. The older we get the more reasons God gives us to seek His comfort. In the end He sends us just enough pain and suffering so that we will want to leave. If everything were perfect, we would never choose to go. He wants us to seek an end to our suffering because He wants us to want to come Home.
Jack McAfghan: Reflections, Chapter 63

ASHES AND MEMORIALS

She took great comfort in holding me. She was holding me in her arms again although she knew perfectly well that I was not In There. The ashes were all she had left of my body but memories of me were everywhere. We had gone everywhere together. Still she clung to that plastic urn of ashes.
Jack McAfghan: Reflections, Chapter 72

There are still decisions that must be made. You probably have guessed by now that it's by design to keep your mind busy. It brings you back in touch with the tangible things of life. It's an important time as there is so much that you otherwise cannot touch and cannot feel and cannot see of me.

Perhaps you will bury me in the garden at home. Maybe you'll have me cremated and when you pick up my ashes you will speak the twilight zone-ish words, "He's back home." Back home in an urn on the altar or upon the hearth. Or perhaps you'll scatter my ashes on a favorite trail, in our dragonfly stream or in the nearby field where flowers dance. It doesn't really matter to me what choice you make because I want you to do what's best for you. It's what you do with your heart that matters the most. I am not in that hole in the ground. I am not in that urn full of ashes.

You are under a great deal of stress. Please take plenty of time to think things through before you make your final arrangements. Consider the long-term possibilities. You must be comfortable if you ever move from the home where my body is buried. If you do move, please do me a favor; don't dig me up as some people do. I am not there. Let what is left of my earthly shell rest in peace.

Scatter my ashes or keep them, whatever is best for you. But if you keep them, please don't cling to them. It is the spirit in which you keep them that makes me happy...or sad...for you and for me. The most important thing is that you are comfortable with the choices that you have made for me. If you are going to remember me, remember me at my best. If you must think about me now, remember me with joy. It's how I lived my life. Remember the way I looked at you when death never entered our minds.

Do not make an altar of my final days or of my pain. Instead, create a treasure box of memories only for my life and the happiness with which I lived it. For the many loves that I had while I was there. There were so many! There was so much everything!

The design of the universe is vast and so is the array of creative memorial options. There are many factors that come into play and so many options to choose from when you wish to memorialize me. There are so many choices it can be overwhelming, but it gives you something to do for yourself in honor of me when you need comfort and care. You don't have to spend a lot of money. If you can live in the moment, you can do everything with clear intention and make it effective for your healing.

One of the simplest things to do is to light a candle for me. Focus on the light and my life. Tea lights are safe and inexpensive. You might put one in a lovely candleholder to create a gentle glow in the darkness of your grief. Be careful however not to create another attachment. If you light a candle every night for me, it becomes another routine that you will one day have to break free from. After all, you would have to light a candle every night for the rest of your life. If you happen to miss one night, you might be filled with guilt and shame and blame that you did not remember to light that candle for me. Losing an attachment, even to something like this, becomes yet another loss. If your life is not complete without the shrine you made for me then you still have me on that leash around my neck. You are still not free, nor am I.

Please don't let go of your love for me, goodness no. Let go of the grief. The need. Learn this as you move forward. The less you cling to something, the less fear you have of losing that something or someone. The less fear you have, the more love you have. It is true that you love even more when you let go of the need for it. Love grows when grief goes. Make your love stronger than your fear. Strive to make your love greater than your need and let love be the most powerful force in your life. Then nothing can overcome you.

You may wish to set up a memorial altar – for my urn, my photo, memorial gifts and cards, my paw print, flowers, collars, tags. Set it up to honor my life, not my death. Celebrate my "Rainbow Birthday" not as the day I died but as the day I was born again. It is cause for celebration for on our rebirth in Heaven we do not come in crying like we do on earth; we come in laughing.

Maybe you will want to make a financial donation in memory of me to a pet-related organization or other charitable group that you wish to support. Donate my personal belongings to a rescue group or animal shelter. It would make me happy to have them used by someone who needs them, rather than storing them in a closet or on a shelf. One of the most personal things is the collar I wore every day. If you took it off of me and still have it, you can donate it to a friend whose dog is outgrowing its puppy collar. Or keep it. Or give it to Goodwill, the Charity Shop or Humane Society store. When I outgrew my first puppy collar, Kate found a nice green collar at the Goodwill to replace it. We always loved that soft faded green collar. I wore it for the rest of my life and we always thanked the dog who had worn it before.

Sometimes carrying something subtle and tangible with you helps to defer anxiety and nervous energy. Put my ID tag on your keychain. You can use it as a comfort stone when you are nervous about something. It can be a reminder during potentially stressful situations that I am there with you. This way you can carry me everywhere and nobody needs to know how you still need to feel me there. It keeps it between you and me.

You must do whatever feels right to you when you feel the time is right for you to do something. There is no hurry. There are no rules. Do we have a garden? Did I love spending time there? Set up an area just for me where you can plant a tree, a rosebush or spread my ashes. Then be sure to observe the space because it is the perfect stage for me to send you signs and messengers!

We learned of a lady who got very ill after eating her husband's ashes. She is not the only one who has done this! I see you are making a face right now, but never judge another's journey. She was desperate to keep him as part of her. She obviously did not believe or have the faith that he would always be a part of her. There are healthier ways to keep my ashes close to you. You can hire an artisan to put them into a piece of jewelry or blend them into a polished crystal. Some will integrate the ashes into a custom tattoo. There are many ways to honor me, ways unique to you and me.

Some communities have pet cemeteries and special events with support for the bereaved. You can have a tree planted in my memory at a local park or hang chimes at a special pet memorial site. Go to our favorite dog park; say hi to our old friends and offer to donate a memorial plaque, a park bench or a tree that gives shade. Give something that will forever honor me and remind of your generosity.

Maybe our veterinarian had the thoughtful foresight to have an imprint of my paw made for you. Such treasured gifts are most welcome right now! Buy yourself something nice in my memory. Whatever suits you. You can even buy a star in the sky and name it after me! I'm Sirius! Consider having a scarf made of my woven hair. Have a photo canvas made of me or hire an artist to paint my portrait. A little angel coin or a worry stone that feels really good to you can be kept in your pocket to touch whenever you need to feel tangibly connected to me. Just try not to cling because in the event you lose that stone, that angel, it becomes another loss to grieve for it is an extension of me that you were hanging onto.

One must be careful not to become dependent on "things" because something can be lost forever seemingly beyond reason, because you were too attached to it. By the losing of it you must then deal with the force of grief in its entirety without the crutch you created for yourself with that sentimental item which you have lost. Grief is designed to help you to learn to stand on your own two feet again...standing without crutches on the legs of your faith.

When you feel up to it, assemble our photos and create a space where you can immerse yourself in my eyes, my fur, and the world that we shared, whenever you wish. Begin to replace the unpleasant memories with memories of better times together.

The tangibles can help you when you are lonely and I am gone from your sight. This way, when you long to touch me, you can touch something that connects you to me through the power of our memory. It's just nice to have something—a stuffed animal, my blanket. You can even find plush animals that you can store my ashes in. Felted animals can be designed to look like me.

A creative project can also be very therapeutic. Make a quilt out of my bandanas. Write a poem. Paint a picture. Create a scrapbook or a collage of our memories. Telling or showing the story about me can be very cathartic and can serve as a memorial tribute that lasts forever. You can also do what Kate did and write something from your pet's perspective, perhaps a letter written from me to you so that you know how much you are loved! Be careful however, for if you tell the story too many times over and over, it can become a habit to the point that you don't know who you are without our story. It only compounds the loss. It makes it one more thing for you to lose: your identity as One Who Grieves. Balance is the key to everything.

When you have learned from something that has brought pain and suffering, when you discover the good that can come of it, you might want to do something that makes a difference to others who are going through the same thing. Some of the greatest works of art, music and literature are the result of deep love and great loss.

LIFE BEYOND GRIEF
LOVING AGAIN

It had been a divine set up. My Master sent me to her to teach her how wonderful it is to love and be loved so that when I was gone from her she would yearn for love again. She would no longer be afraid of love. She would one day realize that the love we shared was her reward for taking a chance on love, for taking a chance on me.
<u>*Return from Rainbow Bridge, Chapter 57*</u>

I see you. I feel your heart. I know why you are lonely. You're lonely because I taught you to love...but you see I couldn't stay forever. I taught you to love because once you love like that you don't know how to live your life without it. I taught you so that you would miss love so much that you would want to find it again. I taught you because I want you to be happy again and to have a beautiful life. I taught you because it's love that makes life worthwhile and if anyone deserves a beautiful life, it's you.

Maybe it doesn't seem fair to you that we do not live a human lifetime. Most of us will come and go in 4 years, 7 years, 12 years, 16, less or more, maybe even 20 if we're lucky. Horses can go a little longer. Maybe you will do

45

this 1 or 2 or 3 more times in your life...if you are willing to risk loving again.

Have you thought about getting another pet? Do you ask yourself: "Can I bear to go through this again? Should I get another pet? If so, when?" Only you know the answer to this. Don't let anyone try to tell you what is best for you. You are the one who knows best. There will always be people who are happy to tell you what they think you should do. What works for one person might not work for another. Do what YOU think you should do.

Early in your grief I heard you announce to others indignantly, "I'm never getting another pet!" I know you said it amidst the deepest pain of your grief, but how do you think that makes me feel? It makes me think that maybe I brought you more pain than joy. If you had me for 15 years and it took three days to lose me, why would you not be willing to love again? Maybe you just aren't up to having a pet right now. Maybe you're too exhausted from the grieving and the growing. Maybe you are still angry. You can always volunteer at a shelter or offer to take care of other people's pets until you have more time to recover. Don't write us off just yet. Based on what you say, you aren't quite healed all the way.

If you want to overcome pain from the past, bring in new life for the future...but only when the time is right. The most important thing you can do is relax about it and Do Not Force Anything. When you are forcing something that doesn't feel right then it isn't right. What is meant to be yours will come.

As you heal you'll feel things begin to shift in your heart. It's my love at work. It's evidence that I am still there with you. You'll find yourself developing stronger relationships with your children and your remaining pets. If you don't have a pet, you might find yourself starting to think about getting another. It is a strange human tendency to feel guilty thinking these thoughts but there is nothing to feel guilty about. It's life. It's loss. It's growth and it's transformation. It's all about love.

Your own voice inside your head will keep you quite busy. "...But it's too soon..." "Won't my old pet be jealous?" "What will people think of me?" "It's just not fair to the others." "My heart tells me YES but my mind says NO." Ah, there's your answer.

If your heart is telling you it's time to love again, listen to it. It always tells the truth. I am in your heart and I am the one who is telling you. With my Heavenly Master's help, I direct the desires of your heart. I direct you so that you are in the right place at the right time for that which is right for you. It may be a week, it may be a year, or less or more. Don't try to judge it or plan it out. I know what you need better than anyone does and I am in the position to bring it to you when you are ready. When the time is right I will guide you to the right one.

I want you to love again. It excites me as I watch you step up to the plate and share the higher love I taught you to give. I want you to love again. Someone who needs you is waiting for you; someone yet unknown who waits patiently but desperately for you, for the love you have in your heart, to give and to receive.

We have a special friend. He has had horses, dogs and cats all of his life since he was a boy down on the family farm. I think the number is 21 pets over the course of his life so far. Every time one dies, he runs out immediately before the shock wears off to get another. Some say he is doing it too soon. Some label him "impulsive." They feel he should take more time to think about it before acting on it. The fact is, he knows what he's doing. It works for him. He doesn't need time to think, he just needs time to feel. He's been through loss enough times to know exactly what he's doing.

"I do it to honor the life of the one I just lost," he says. Imagine if he were still deliberating whether or not to get another pet. He would never have had 21 rounds of love stories with no doubt more to come, God willing. Pets can keep their best two-legged friends healthier longer. Aside from obvious social perks, pets are good for the heart, the blood pressure, depression prevention and stress relief.

I am not telling you that this is how you should do it because everyone is different.

What I will ask of you is to consider adopting another pet when the time is right for you, because it will honor me. Because I'm the one who taught you how to love more than you ever did before.

"Don't you think I am too old for another pet?" you ask.

Geraldine was 90. She had lost her only daughter and lived alone at home with her 10-year-old Shih Tzu. They were the best of friends but when her dog passed unexpectedly, Geri immediately called Kate to help her locate a new pet. They found Buddy, a three-year old poodle that had been abused, turned into the kill shelter and then saved by a local rescue group. The two had shared three wonderful years together when Geri had to say goodbye to Buddy when she went into hospice care. She predeceased him.

Because of Geri's willingness to love again and again, she had had 30 pets over her 90 years. 30 hellos, 30 goodbyes, and 30 more angels waiting for her at the edge of the Rainbow Bridge. Buddy now lives very comfortably with Geri's best friend. It worked out really well because Geri and Buddy and her friend always spent so much time together that it was quite easy for Buddy to adjust to it all after Geri was gone. Please don't hesitate to get another pet no matter what your age. Just plan ahead so that you have someone nearby to help when you can't do it all and who will be happy to take them into their home if you are taken home to Heaven first.

Geri knew. Each and every pet is different and you can never replace a pet with a new one and have the same experience you had before. That's the beauty of it. Each pet teaches you new kinds of lessons and each lesson is always about a new kind of love.

You are never too old to love again. In fact you have more to offer than ever, based on the wisdom of your years. Just make your choices wisely based on who you are now. If you have trouble walking around the block, don't get a hound that needs a lot of exercise unless you have a big fenced-in yard. Get a lapdog or a cat that can get plenty of exercise just running around the house or on a slow and gentle walk through the neighborhood. Consider a 7-pound pet rather than a 70-pound pet. Keep your eyes open for a five-year-old not a five-month-old. Be sure, like Geri did, to put a plan in your will that includes directives where your new pet will go if you die first.

You think I'll be upset if you live to love again?
Why, I came here to teach you love! What good
is learning something if you never use it?
I'm asking you to love again.
Return from Rainbow Bridge Chapter 87

I know you are still grieving the loss of me. I know that I was your very best friend. I want you to be happy above all and somewhere there is someone else who needs you. So many are waiting for a good home like the one you gave to me. They are waiting in shelters and foster homes. Perfectly healthy loving pets are facing their final hours in kill shelters. You could make a difference in the life of the one who needs you. The one who is waiting for love to walk through the door. Waiting to be chosen. Waiting to surprise you with how much love they have to give to you.

As you wait for your new friend to come into your life, never ever try to duplicate me for you will be dealt a hand you never planned on. When you try to keep things the "same," you will be given a whole new set of challenges. You will look at the one who looks like me and say, "Why can't you be more like ___?" because when they look like me you subconsciously expect them to act like me and they are not me. It is not fair to yourself or to your new pet. Plus, think about it from my point of view. "Is she trying to replace me?" Just no. Same breed is okay. If you HAPPEN to fall in love with one that HAPPENS to resemble me, well, okay. Let your heart lead the way, not your eyes and your desire to keep things the same.

I am not where you are looking. Don't agonize about it. The pet that's meant to be with you will simply arrive at the right time. You'll find yourself in the right place. You'll feel the certainty in your heart. That's how you'll know it will be yours.

There is something that tends to happen for many of you. Sometimes you think you've found the right one. You fall in love quickly. You are sure this is The One. Oh you can hardly wait to start this new chapter of love! Scared and excited, you find yourself already quite attached to them. Then something happens and it doesn't work out. You cry because you have invested so much of yourself in this process. You were so sure! You say "Why?"

Why? Because that one did you a favor. These are your teachers too. They were put in your life by design. They either led you to the Right One that you would not have found otherwise, or they healed something inside of you that still needed healing before you could be ready to commit to love again. Do not judge what seems to be unfortunate. It is by design. The heart guides you every step of the way. We guide you. We know exactly what you need and when.

Try not to feel guilty for another moment about this. I am not jealous. I love you and my love is true. All I want is for you to be happy again. I don't want you to feel alone anymore.

When new love comes to you I will not envy because I know that no one takes my place with you. I'm in your heart and there I'll stay. I'll wait without condition and I will love the ones you come to love.
<u>*Jack McAfghan: Reflections, Chapter 88*</u>

When you have healed you'll be more confident and you will find yourself willing to take some risks again. I can feel you saying now, "No, no, no. I don't want to take anymore risks..." You aren't quite ready but when the moment comes I want you to remember the risks you have taken that have made your life better. I want you to remember the risk that you took that very first day when you brought me into your home and your heart.

You ask, "When...When will the crying end? When will the grieving end? When will I look at my new pet and not just miss the one I used to have?"

Believe me when I tell you this. It will just take a little time and you will one day find that all your loves have merged together. You will be surprised because you will find yourself laughing or smiling over a memory of me and that's when you will know that your tears will soon subside. I want you to be free to love again and to be happy when you are reminded of me! You'll get there, you'll see, and it will be sweet and beautiful with a few sentimental tears now and again for all the loves you have had.

ALL THE LOVE YOU EVER GAVE
WAITS FOR YOU AT RAINBOW BRIDGE.

THE END
is just the BEGINNING....

Death is like turning the final page in a book you've come to love. This is a love story that never ends. It's never over. You and me.
Heart to Heart.

Neither death nor life, neither angels nor demons, neither our fears for today nor our worries about tomorrow—not even the powers of hell can separate us.
Romans 8:38

WHEN SOMEONE YOU LOVE IS DYING

<u>Tell them you love them</u> love them love them.

<u>Acknowledge what is happening now</u>. They need someone to share in their experience of Life's Final Stage of Growth.

<u>Let them know in no uncertain terms that they are free to go.</u> Be sure to tell them you will miss them.

<u>Thank them for all they did for you</u> – even if it was to teach you patience, tolerance or not to take things personally.

<u>Ask them to send you a sign</u> after they get where they're going. Ask them to come into your dreams or tell them some other specific way you would like them to show up in your life.

If they are nearing death, <u>prioritize them</u>. Take time off from work. Cancel your dates, your family vacation. This will help you to relieve the guilt that always comes when they are gone.

<u>Live in the moment with them</u>. Put your smartphone away. Look into their eyes even if you have never done that before in your life together with them. It is the eyes that hold the memories of the soul.

<u>Communicate with them from your heart</u>. When they are gone from your sight it is not your mouths and your ears but your hearts that will communicate one to the other.

<u>Remind yourself that they are not "dead."</u> They live on in another form in another place not far from you.

<u>BLESS THEM AND LET THEM GO.</u>

RESOURCES

If you struggle with grief and loss, please seek out a qualified bereavement/loss counselor to help you. Most local hospice organizations have a trained social worker or chaplain available who provides services to the community at low or no charge. National Volunteer Agencies can also help. Consider reading our other Jack McAfghan books, for each one heals your heart in a different way.

**We invite you to join Jack's group
for online support and TLC:**
Healing Pet Loss Heart to Heart
www.facebook.com/groups/edgeoftherainbow

Interact with Jack on Facebook:
www.facebook.com/MyJackofHearts

Visit Kate
www.facebook.com/KateMcGahanAuthor
www.katemcgahan.com

Find all of Kate and Jack's books here:
author.to/BooksByKateMcGahan
or on her website www.katemcgahan.com

OTHER BOOKS IN THE SERIES

The Jack McAfghan Pet Loss Trilogy

Jack McAfghan: Reflections
A Dog's Memoir on Life After Death
Start healing your heart by the final page.
Our story is your story too.

The Lizard from Rainbow Bridge
The True Tale of an Unexpected Angel
Learn to recognize the afterlife signs that
are all around you.

Jack McAfghan's Return from Rainbow Bridge
An Afterlife Story of Love, Loss and Renewal
Open your mind to the possibilities that
exist in life after death.

~~~~~~

Only Gone from Your Sight: Jack
McAfghan's Little Guide to Pet Loss & Grief
The international best-selling guide to grief
recovery which includes all of the chapters in the
book you are holding right now ---and much more!

Letters from Rainbow Bridge: Answers to Your
Questions About Pet Loss & the Afterlife
Jack answers reader's letters, addressing
questions about death and the afterlife.

Kate and Jack

Kate McGahan has been a hospice counselor and clinical social worker for 35 years and now lives in Southern Arizona. She has a Bachelor's Degree in Social Work from Nazareth College of Rochester and a Master's Degree in Social Work from Syracuse University. She began writing the Jack McAfghan Series of books in 2015 after experiencing the loss of her dog, Jack, and she has more books and genres forthcoming. Kate brings her stories to her readers in an entertaining and thought-provoking way. When you learn something new you grow, when you grow you heal. It's By Design. Bringing a lifetime of experience and clinical expertise into each and every book, Kate seeks to heal something in each and every reader.

Intensely spiritual and highly intuitive, Kate sprinkles the subtle seeds of faith to strengthen the reader's spiritual path. While you think she is just entertaining you, she is continually teaching you new ways of looking at yourself and those you love.

Godspeed Your Journey ♥

Made in United States
North Haven, CT
04 March 2023